Don't panic.

Postcard

Today's a new day!

Postcard

From *Good Morning and Good Night* by Jane Werner,
illustrated by Eloise Wilkin, 1949.

Get some exercise every day.

Postcard

From *Animal Gym* by Beth Greiner Hoffman,
illustrated by Tibor Gergely, 1956.

Frolic.

Postcard

From *Tootle* by Gertrude Crampton,
illustrated by Tibor Gergely, 1945.

Daydream.

Postcard

Stargaze.

Postcard

From *The Friendly Book* by Margaret Wise Brown,
illustrated by Garth Williams, 1954.

Stroll.

Postcard

From *The Three Bears*, illustrated by Feodor Rojankovsky, 1948.

Bird-watch.

Postcard

From *I Am a Bunny*, A Golden Sturdy Book, by Ole Risom, illustrated by Richard Scarry, 1963.

The simplest things are often the most fun!

Postcard

From *The Saggy Baggy Elephant* by Kathryn and Byron Jackson, illustrated by Gustaf Tenggren, 1947.

Make music a part of your life.

Postcard

From *The Musicians of Bremen*,
adapted from Jacob and Wilhelm Grimm,
illustrated by J. P. Miller, 1954.

Use your imagination.

Postcard

From *Nurse Nancy* by Kathryn Jackson,
illustrated by Corinne Malvern, 1952.

Take in some culture once in a while.

Postcard

Learn something new!

Postcard

From *Tootle* by Gertrude Crampton,
illustrated by Tibor Gergely, 1945.

**Dare to explore.
What's out there
for you?**

Postcard

From *The Sailor Dog* by Margaret Wise Brown,
illustrated by Garth Williams, 1953.

Try a new look!

Postcard

From *Pantaloon* by Kathryn Jackson,
illustrated by Leonard Weisgard, 1951.

Be unique.

Postcard

From *Rupert the Rhinoceros* by Carl Memling,
illustrated by Tibor Gergely, 1960.

Start planning that dream trip!

Postcard

From *Open Up My Suitcase* by Alice Low,
illustrated by Corinne Malvern, 1954.

Keep in touch.

Postcard

From *Seven Little Postmen*
by Margaret Wise Brown and Edith Thacher Hurd,
illustrated by Tibor Gergely, 1952.

Steer clear of shady characters.

Postcard

From *Chicken Little*, adapted by Vivienne Benstead,
illustrated by Richard Scarry, 1960.

Don't forget your antioxidants!

Postcard

From *The Color Kittens* by Margaret Wise Brown,
illustrated by Alice and Martin Provensen, 1949.

Dress up and go dancing.

Postcard

From *The Twelve Dancing Princesses* by the Brothers Grimm, retold by Jane Werner, illustrated by Sheilah Beckett, 1954.

Make something from nothing.

Postcard

From *The Party Pig* by Kathryn and Byron Jackson,
illustrated by Richard Scarry, 1954.

Cultivate contentment.

Postcard

From *Tawny Scrawny Lion* by Kathryn Jackson,
illustrated by Gustaf Tenggren, 1952.

**Take a mental health day
now and then.**

Postcard

From *The Little Red Hen*, illustrated by J. P. Miller, 1954.

**Remember to stop and
smell the strawberries.**

Postcard

From *The Poky Little Puppy* by Janette Sebring Lowrey,
illustrated by Gustaf Tenggren, 1942.

Be a romantic.

Postcard

From *The Blue Book of Fairy Tales*,
illustrated by Gordon Laite, 1959.

Play hard.

Postcard

From *Mister Dog* by Margaret Wise Brown,
illustrated by Garth Williams, 1952.

Do no harm.

Postcard

From *My Little Golden Book About God* by Jane Werner Watson, illustrated by Eloise Wilkin, 1956.

Think big!

Postcard

Toot your own horn!

Postcard

From *Little Boy with a Big Horn* by Jack Bechdolt,
illustrated by Aurelius Battaglia, 1950.